Waiting for an Etcher

Waiting for an Etcher

Chip Dameron

Copyright © 2015 Chip Dameron
All Rights Reserved

ISBN: 978-0-9915321-8-6
Library of Congress Control Number: 2015931100

Front Cover Etching by James Abbott McNeill Whistler
Manufactured in the United States

Lamar University Press
Beaumont, Texas

For my son, Michael

Poetry from Lamar University Press

Alan Berecka, *With Our Baggage*
David Bowles, *Flower, Song, Dance*: Aztec *and Mayan Poetry* (a new translation)
Jerry Bradley, *Crownfeathers and Effigies*
William Virgil Davis, *The Bones Poems*
Jeffrey DeLotto, *Voices Writ in Sand*
Mimi Ferebee, *Wildfires and Atmospheric Memories*
Ken Hada, *Margaritas and Redfish*
Michelle Hartman, *Disenchanted and Disgruntled*
Katherine Hoerth, *Goddess Wears Cowboy Boots*
Lynn Hoggard, *Motherland*
Gretchen Johnson, *A Trip Through Downer, Minnesota*
Janet McCann, *The Crone at the Casino*
Erin Murphy, *Ancilla*
Dave Oliphant, *The Pilgrimage, Selected Poems: 1962-2012*
Carol Coffee Reposa, *Underground Mucicians*
Jan Seale, *The Parkinson Poems*
Carol Smallwood, *Water, Earth, Air, Fire, and Picket Fences*

For information on these and other Lamar University Press books go to www.LamarUniversityPress.Org

Acknowledgments

The author gratefully acknowledges the following journals and anthologies in which some of these poems first appeared.

Additional Studies in Rio Grande Valley History
Boundless 2012
Boundless 2013
Boundless 2014
Boyne Berries
Full Circle
Journal of South Texas English Studies
Leaf Press
Mesquite Review
New Border Voices: An Anthology
San Antonio Express-News
San Pedro River Review
Southern Ocean Review
Voices of Hellenism Literary Journal
Writer's Bloc Literary Magazine

CONTENTS

Along the Border

- 15 Across
- 16 Dinner Hour
- 17 And Old Guerrero Waits
- 18 Border Birding
- 19 Afternoon of Gifts
- 20 Fledglings
- 21 Grackles in Molt
- 22 Cormorants
- 23 Who Cooks for You?
- 24 Poem in October
- 25 Rambling Stories
- 26 Semantics
- 27 Viewpoints, Early Summer
- 28 Cave of Air
- 29 Ides of March
- 30 Hurricane Season
- 31 Grief Afloat
- 32 Waiting for an Etcher

On the Roadside

- 35 Drought Season
- 36 Drought's End
- 37 Vantage Point
- 38 Flags of Dominion
- 39 Roadside Eden

Changes of Place

- 43 Hot Night Tale in Little Rock
- 44 Note from New Orleans
- 45 Lost in the Funhouse
- 46 Visit to Wolf House
- 47 On Cold Mountain
- 48 Bloomsday

49 The Amateur
50 Giacometti Park
51 Lisbon Lingo
52 Oculus
53 Cold Comfort
54 Firenze's Grand Illusion
55 Delphi
56 Istanbul's Museum of Innocence

Postcards

59 In Sligo
60 In Connemara
61 Galway Gal
62 In Dublin
63 Sidewalk in Dingle Town
64 Dingle Ogham Stones
65 In La Seyne sur Mer
66 In Bern
67 In Munich
68 Near Florence
69 In Venice
70 In Bolzano
71 Athens Artist
72 At Meteora
73 On the Aegean Sea
74 Portara at Naxos
75 Naxos Hike
76 Santorini Sunset
77 Santorini Concertina
78 In Amorgos
79 John at Patmos
80 Istanbul Selfie
81 Istanbul Mosques

Tributes

85 El Calaboz: Fences and Neighbors
86 Brutus Abroad

87	Aftershock
88	For Glen Sorestad
89	Portrait at Frank's Place
90	Travels with Marko
91	*Raymonda*, 1975
93	Umpteenth Operation
94	December Walk with Gene
95	Billy Collins and Garrison Keillor in the Poetry Ring

Gravity's End

99	Rescuing Strangers from the Dead
100	These Brittle Prints
101	Christmas Tree Rings
102	Lasting Gift
103	Inventory for Moving 1
104	Inventory for Moving 2
105	Final Song
106	Omen
107	Visit Back Home
108	Holy Chihuly!
109	Mama Buddha
110	On the Third Floor

Along the Border

Across

Across the river is another version of your life,
the smells sharper along the streets,
the same heat somehow hotter, more humid,
air filtered through bursts of words
that open at first but soon close down,
their metallic surfaces of sound
a form of music rather than speech.
A man drinking coffee in a corner café
has been waiting, still waits, for you
to open the door and say what you
have often felt the need to say,
however halting and inexact it may be.

Dinner Hour

Ribs on the grill, reefs of cloud
across the ribbon lake redden
above the trees, then pink to gray
and drain the last of the light
as egrets flap toward roosts
and night defies the citronella's fumes,
the buzz and bite no longer
just irritants, the dengue fever
aching bones and taking lives
south of the river, while here
in paradise we swat and wipe off
the blood and order death
to stay away awhile longer.

And Old Guerrero Waits

When you flood a town
you'd better fill the lake
deeper than the memories
of those who lived there,
even the ones in the graves
not moved because no one
knew about them any more.
Whispers keep bubbling up
to the surface and words
break against the bows
of pleasure boats and fishing
skiffs. Here basements and cisterns
and rat holes have swallowed
an engineer's wealth of water
and thrust roofs and spires
sunward, waiting for the curious
to come for a visit and
stay for a long long time.

Border Birding

Birds stream across
from the south

while men and
women still dodge

river thieves and
wade murky currents

balancing their bundles
as green cousins

binocular the banks
clip their wings

and send them
back in cages.

Afternoon of Gifts

Intruding on talk about baseball memories
and Mexican cartel-flavored bus adventures
and Grossman's novel on damaged
Israelis and their Muslim shadows,
the polite eavesdropper speaks
of his Palestinian girlfriend, born
in Kuwait, medically trained in Latvia,
aiming to immigrate to Canada,
while he, ex-Marine, will soon
return to lucrative contract work
in Afghanistan or Iraq. He pulls
out a handcrafted souvenir, a metal
keychain missing its keys,
a faceless form joined to the daggered
landscape of Israel, Arabic lettering
along one side, and gives it
as a memento to our chance exchange
in a Texas border coffee shop,
center of a narrowing universe.

Fledglings

If we'd gone by in a car we would have missed it.
Even bikes would have likely pulled us spinning past.

The woman waiting for a phone call in the breezy
front yard shade, pointing out a nest in a nearby tree.

The bobbing news photographer's head in the makeshift
two-story blind, bent on immortalizing first flight.

The offered binoculars, the flurry of a kiskadee flycatcher,
perched at the nest's side hole, feeding the fledglings.

The husband coming out of the door, retired shrimper
turned fish-and-wildlife hand, pleased to talk of doves

and 28 years of planting trees and composting leaves,
sounding like the Cajun he's not, his wife says.

Next time we go by by bike or car we'll remember
the lemon breast, the man's grin, the deep shade.

Grackles in Molt

The yard's dotted
with small
black ducks

sharp beaks
pointed toward
heaven

as if
tail feathers
will fall

and make
the balance
they've lacked.

Cormorants

They sit six across the wire
fence that stops abruptly
fifteen feet into the resaca,
facing the current that ripples
from the south, wings slightly
open, watching the movie
of life unfold. As the afternoon
lengthens, their baritone clacks
reverberate, and when long
shadows tell them it's time,
one dives off and bounces
toward liftoff, then another
and another, all six now
lining their way to the night's
roost, leaving me to wait
for the final credits to end.

Who Cooks for You?

So ask the white-winged doves,
a dozen or so around the neighborhood,
calls crisscrossing the morning light,
cutting through the house sparrows' chitter.

I know they aren't addressing me,
but the question deserves its answer:
from mother and wife to good friends,
from swanky chefs to café fry cooks.

These words have been nourished
by countless daily kindnesses, giving
bees their backbone, ems their length,
esses their languid, supple sauciness.

Cu cu ca choo?
Who cooks for you?

Poem in October

The molting grackles roam the campus lawn,
on loan from their roosts and their skyways
to tomorrow. Cooped inside, looking out,
I wish that I could shed coat and tie
and absorb the cottonwood's leaves
against the clotted sky, the south wind
stirring the day and taking time
on its undulating back as it did
long ago in a boy's backyard,
summer gone, the days cooling,
the light sparkling with the sounds
of a young neighborhood, tomorrow
a place on the other side of the world,
full of all the energies of that moment.

Rambling Stories

As we walked one winter morning
through your neighborhood and took
the new hike and bike trail
toward downtown, we soon found
ourselves on a country road
in Ireland, hearing McGahern's people
repeat close-held prejudices amidst
the evidence of change, and then
we hiked up a mountain village
in Gage's northwest Greece and hid
in a cave, the Nazis now gone
but teenage boys and girls forced
into comradeship, *andartes* and
andartinas sent to stop the royalists'
bullets, and next we walked along
a wet street in the Istanbul dark,
holding an unfamiliar object that
might be a clue to another of Pamuk's
Byzantine mysteries, but before
we could establish its talismanic
meaning we had reached our destination,
a small downtown café, and as Larry
the owner refilled our coffee cups
he told us stories of his days
in the merchant marine, his childhood
in rural western North Carolina,
his string of wives, his ninth grade
education, his thirst for books, and
his town's intolerance toward outsiders—
*we'd send a couple of the boys
to kick their butts*—and he smiled
as he looked across the counter
at his Mexican wife and ticked off
successes of children and step-children
in this border town that has taken
him in and let him talk and talk.

Semantics

TV newscast at six: *Last night
an elderly woman, age 62,
was struck by a car and died.*
Not touched directly by this trauma
in a nearby border town, I wonder
instead when a woman or man
officially becomes *elderly*: old,
failing, largely ineffectual.
Some clans speak of *elders*
instead, those tempered souls
who tell vital stories, tell
a watch dog from a wolf.
At 65, on long walks along
neighborhood streets, I guard
against distracted drivers, monitor
my trick knee, and listen to ducks
whistle overhead, then disappear
like arrows into the blue beyond
the rooftops, unsponsored and
unmoved by human definitions.

Viewpoints, Early Summer

The wrinkled skin
of the oxbow lake

takes the north breeze
toward dusk, as

grackles cross from
trees to brush

and punctuate air
with their clacks

and chirrs, their
piercing circus whistles.

A neighbor glides
by in a kayak,

shoulders sun-reddened,
heading for home.

The prayer flags
flutter on the patio,

five fading reminders
of the Chinese frontier,

their runic sounds
still muzzled.

Cave of Air

Within the live oak's open limbs
a cave of air beckons us

to spring forth and trust
our vestigial wings, make

a nest of wind and sunlight,
and replicate the lonely sounds

that call forth the moon
when night is long and cloudy

and only the crickets seem
to care if anyone's still awake.

Ides of March

Even when the wind blows
hour after hour, dry as an open mouth,

people think their cars will return
from the mall or the office to their homes,

night might bring coolness and closure,
something might pry loose the roof

of the world and lave their lives with wet
smells and sounds and fits of laughter,

and when your eyes glisten in the rain
I forget what the wind seemed to say.

Hurricane Season

We're due a big blow one day soon,
waiting in our arc of the gulf for what
comes roiling forth from offshore Africa.

We have communal sins enough—overbuilt
barrier island, drug traffic, sprawling
colonias—to warrant a god's cleansing scour,

but the hour will come when wind
and current and heat meet in an unplanned
dance that spins to its own ancient howl.

Grief Afloat

I go by canoe round the bend
of the resaca, and there above
the trees a star winks its red eye
and glows like an unfamiliar porch light.

*You can drift along all night
and all the next day, but you
aren't going to find what you're
looking for, are you?*

Maybe not. But I'm hoping
to hear something in the dark
that tells me how to keep on
living beyond her dying.

*The answer is there is no answer.
Every paddle stroke, every breath
you take makes up your living.
What you do is who you are.*

I steer for the bank and pull
the canoe into the grass. Night is giving
way and the bright star is gone.
I take one step, then another, toward home.

Waiting for an Etcher

Night steals in
with its memories
of early love and
somebody's death

you hear a crow
call out in fear
and you smell
coyote coming nearer

but when you wake
the light turns
crow to grackle
coyote to cat

love's just a shadow
and death ah death
an image on glass
waiting for an etcher.

On the Roadside

Drought Season

Sunhead has been out so long
his wrinkles have grown wrinkles.

Rainhead keeps her long blue hair
pulled up in a tight bun.

Moonhead goes from dreamer to dreamer
with her pitcher of spring water.

Windhead hears every dry rumor
and passes the best on.

Stumphead remembers how wet smelled:
waves of weed breath and road stink.

Drought's End

Thunder gave Stumphead's rain-swollen
head a good reason to ache,

the cracking air unrolling shock
after shock, battering his brain.

His thoughts had come to be
so dry, rooted in the parched dirt

of the desiccated roadside
for all this spring and summer,

and now his head so wet
day after day his thoughts

were like the tangle of vines
along the nearby fence, curling

as they uncoiled and intermingled,
a greeny riot swelling toward

the sun, taking him by surprise
to places drenched with wonder.

Vantage Point

Stumphead knows what happens on his road,
what happens on his side of the road:

cars back and forth, tires and asphalt
in steady whine over shared frictions;

cups and bottles offered to the weeds;
lots of eyes at night, sometimes blood

and skunk stink there to greet Sunhead.
Up the road, Hillhead sees even more:

where things come from and go to.
Enough to give Stumphead's roots an itch.

Flags of Dominion

The road held cars, the fence held cattle.
Sunhead said so, Moonhead too.

Stumphead was as patriotic as another.
The flapping barbed-wire flags talked

of dominion: things on the earth
and in the air bound to listen up.

Stumphead wished he had a role:
as lookout, maybe, or presidential guard,

dependable as dawn and stubborn enough
to hold the same view forever.

There between the fence and road,
weeds spread and litter took root.

The day of the big storm, Windhead
tore the flags away and flung them

into the far trees, where Stumphead
liked to think one might still be flying.

Roadside Eden

Roadside and fieldside, the wildflower invasion
spread like flames and scorched the spring to life.

Cars came by and gawked, yet Stumphead felt
invisible, half pink from Indian paintbrush.

One day one stopped and a young girl got out
and picked her way from clump to clump.

Snakehead waited in a bush against the fence,
watching the shape bobbing toward him,

the girl shouting toward his face, "Here's a *new* one!"
One step before his strike she turned to her

mother's call and reluctantly retreated, holding
the batch of stems with care in one fist.

Sundown came, Snakehead searched for food.
One day, he thought, *one day she'll be back.*

Changes of Place

Hot Night Tale in Little Rock

Friday night, Texas League ball
at the red brick park just waiting
across the street: we skipped
our evening program, were given

three tickets by a kind local
at the gate, then settled down
with hot dogs and cold beer
and cheered on the home team

as if we knew the shortstop's
shortcomings, the pitcher's best
pitch, the way a double down
the left-field line caroms out

of the corner: on we listened
to the narrative's thwack and pop
and sizzle, the story we've known
by heart since we were kids,

sitting in the stands with our dads,
damp with humid hope, willing
for the game to go on as long
as it took to come to the right ending.

Note from New Orleans

The hole in the wet bracing air that you left
when you returned home has filled with sunlight,
warm with coffee and beignets among the pigeons
and Japanese tourists by Jackson Square.

A grizzled trumpeter hawks his band's gospel tape
to a captive cafe audience, and the street clown
still twists balloons into animals for passers by.

If you were here today, I would commandeer
a carriage and we'd clatter upriver, past
the fields and barges, and when we tired
we'd stop at some town and find the horse
a home and fill ourselves with bowls of file gumbo.

Lost in the Funhouse

Cheap drinks, cheap food, bright blues and oranges
and neon parrots selling an air-conditioned paradise—

a huge man chews down pizza slices one after another
and his heavy wife plucks toppings from a whole pizza

and stuffs them into her mouth, sucking her fingers
and watching her two skinny boys race around the tables,

while in the gaming rooms, where the banks of slot machines
glow and spin their dials under the garish lights,

a woman feeds one a token and presses a big square button,
feeds in another and another and another,

ready to do this all night long to hear the clatter
of coins in the payoff trough, partly refilling her bucket,

and a man sits with his stacks of chips at a blackjack table,
cigarette angled at the corner of his mouth, squinting

at the cards that mean he's lousy or unlucky,
the upbeat piped-in music urging him to go again,

while another chartered bus from Texas or upstate Louisiana
arrives, and everyone troops in for the promise of unending fun.

Visit to Wolf House

Despite posted warnings, no rattlesnakes
sine waved across the dirt path leading
to Jack London's folly, stones stacked
around imagined rooms, a glorious ruin
with a weed-choked reflecting pool
in a dry country far from the wet gums
of the sea. The real story of the walk
on the way in was the woman coming
down a hill alongside her two kids
and mother, grinning in the sunlight,
stabbing the earth with her walking stick
as she flung a leg up and out and down,
bound to finish the mile-and-a-half round trip
to the house and grave, her palsy no bar
to her joy and the day of her joy.

On Cold Mountain

Clouds hide nine ridges of the range.
Young honeymooners laze in the other cabin
behind the hazy scrim of trees.
A rabbit crosses the gravel road
that a cat hunted along last night.
Slowly the ridges emerge
as the sun burns forth the day.

Warm walking across the meadow
and down to the homesteads below,
the layered peaks clusters of green tree life.
Crows exchange their caws.

Thunder tumbles along the range.
Rain peppers the tin roof, eases,
then starts a steady drumbeat.
Fog boils up from the hollows
as if from steaming springs.
Peaks disappear and return
and slowly vanish again.

After dusk, we listen to the rain
as we read of other worlds,
then drift into mountain dreaming.

Bloomsday

Pale summer light dimples the Liffey,
Monday traffic streams along the quays,
a dozen cranes redefine the skyline,
and somewhere Molly is saying yes
again and again, the tourists clapping
and then dispersing to pubs and shops,
the locals about their ordinary rounds,
grown past the outrage and rejection,
glad now to claim the pen that sketched
their narrow consciences once, before
the smart jobs and second homes
in the west, before the Polish waitresses
and Bangladeshi porters, Joyce's
bespectacled face affixed to tee shirts
and kitchen magnets, briskly sold
for too many euros, home at last,
the annual wake one way to make
a long day recover their prodigal son.

The Amateur

Up and down the rolling Wicklows
south of Dublin, purple heather
leading to summery blue lakes
and a cemetery with German crosses,
the seasoned van driver pauses
to pull out his ash hurling stick,
bouncing a small stitched ball
off the flattened toe, taped and nicked,
telling of boys at four or five
with shortened sticks, first games
at ten or eleven, the best of them
playing out their twenties as amateurs—
no padding, seldom serious injuries—
"You have to control yourself, or
you'll never be playing again," he says,
gnarled fingers gripping the handle,
wrists ready to crack another score.

Giacometti Park

Inside the pocket park
in an old Montparnasse
neighborhood, a few locals
stretch across the grass,
soaking up memories against
the coming gray months.

Later we return, find
a quiet bench, open sacks,
and share a round
of country bread, some
Camembert, a chocolate bar,
two bottles of water.

As day darkens, we pass
a mixed foursome of youths
pretending to play boules,
then make our way back,
absorbed by the city
of lights, still in love.

Lisbon Lingo

The eucalyptus seeds along the walkway
were big as lug nuts, inscribed in perfect
runic symmetry—this one a three-spoke wheel,
that one a cross, the last a star—
as if thousands of years of drama
along the Tagus and beyond the sea
had been compressed into these buttons
of time gathered from the graveled dirt.

When I offered them to a boy
passing by, he gave me an *obrigado*
and then tossed them one by one
at an impish girl who dodged them
as he chased the laughter that
disappeared around the corner,
her laughter telling another tale,
deeper even than those others.

Oculus

I would have wished for rain—
fruitful weeping for a green spring—
but took in the fabled light,
the vital eye of Hadrian's god,
surviving waves of plunder
and Catholic churchification,
undoing what we'd like to know
one ring at a time, spinning
in marbled steadiness, fresh
with the sounds of a day
that will soon cast a last
shadow for the coming night,
the moon rising once again
and winking eye for eye.

Cold Comfort

From the station in the valley,
take the funicular to the top
of the volcanic tuft to Orvieto.
If it is bitter to the bone, wind
scouring the streets of sightseers,
let the Duomo pull you in
to thaw and perhaps be saved,
for the moment, then hurry down
the crooked street to a narrow
refuge with bowls of steaming soup
and plates of pasta with cinghiale,
the head of a wild boar beckoning
beside the entrance, red wine just
fortifying the blood for the descent.

Firenze's Grand Illusion

Along the pavement by the Accademia,
local hustlers lay out illegal prints,
tempting Michelangelo's fan club
while watching for police scooters,
the daily cat-and-mouse attention
to life on the street, while David
waits inside, cold and glorious,
his bare haunches celebrating all
it means to be nearly flawless, as
each in the crowd moves slowly
around his graceful gravity and on
to another room, still absorbing
the marbled confidence of a boy
larger than any biblical Goliath.

Delphi

As I walk past the world-centering
omphalos and take in tiered ruins

on Parnassus's fragrant slope,
where no Pythia now inhales

the fabled trance-inducing
fumes while priests interpret

her ecstatic raving, I think of
Alexander, impatient to make

his indelible mark, grabbing her
by the hair until she blurted

out "invincible," then striding
off past the waves of poppies,

their bright-red throats clotted
with black crosses, toward

a future that would prove
to be fatally unpredictable.

Istanbul's Museum of Innocence

In this most intimate of spaces,
spiraling up from a wall of lipsticked

cigarette butts to hundreds of photos
of old Istanbul, news clippings,

vintage watches, ceramic TV dogs,
and a single earring, I catch

Füsun's scent, display by display,
and Kemal Bey's indefatigable ardor,

finally atomized in the spare penthouse
of his final days, slippers at rest,

and I know I've located Füsun's
truest lover, there in the Turkish script

of notebook pages along the wall,
words of creative innocence and guilt.

Postcards

In Sligo

I've here come to
remember Yeats

and spotted a poem
on the Garavogue

a mute swan
carving blue sounds.

In Connemara

Turf stacked
in a rumpled field

clouds lean down
to kiss the ben

the road ahead
disappears.

Galway Gal

Featured trad show star
Emma turns up dancing

on a wooden box on Shop Street
for change, loose limbed

and smiling, reclaiming a style
older than stiff stepping.

In Dublin

I looked
everywhere

for Molly
but only found

skyline cranes
in bloom.

Sidewalk in Dingle Town

That's Robert Mitchum's star
by Dick Mack's hardware store and pub

one old timer, leading tours
of beehive huts and monasteries, says

"We truly hope we aren't visited
anytime soon by *Ryan's Granddaughter*."

Dingle Ogham Stones

Four lichen-splotched
sentinels now line

Lord Ventry's drive
we dumbly ponder

their hash-marked
megalithic whispers.

In La Seyne sur Mer

Train from Paris: our first encounter
with Joan's maternal clan

grandmother, uncles, aunts, cousins
a feast al fresco of pasta, lamb

red wine from backyard vines
sun turning blood into bonds.

In Bern

Those fabled bears
were confined

centuries ago
but the museum

can't tame Klee's
demonic whimsies.

In Munich

Hitler's beer hall
crawls with tourists,

loud Sunday locals,
steins and hot plates

no one here wants
to think about the past.

Near Florence

Down the hill
from Fiesole

early light unwraps
Brunelleschi's dome

as if it were cooling
into striped candy.

In Venice

As tourists wander
about the square

a seagull sits atop
St. Mark's lion's head

cleans a webbed foot
and gazes skyward.

In Bolzano

In August the only
mummy is Otzi

frozen for 3,000 years
at dusk teens chill out

by the bridge and wait
for their lives to harden.

Athens Artist

Months after her grandmother died,
Fanny recreated her lemon trees,

pale yellow and soft green
globes and ovals, and hovering

upper left are the cascading
filaments of her fateful spirit.

At Meteora

These cave-pocked conglomerate
peaks, towering like Olympian

stalagmites, lured monks who scrapped
and scrabbled and constructed

monasteries as if perched halfway
between holy and human.

On the Aegean Sea

It almost makes you want
to believe again in the gods—

Poseidon's royal blue mantle
dominating the azure sky,

the islands on the horizon
calling out our old Greek names.

Portara at Naxos

Apollo gazes northwest
through the massive doorway

toward his sun-dazed Delos island.
Dionysus looks southeast

where the rocky ridge
shields his rich valley vineyards.

Naxos Hike

We find the huge, unfinished
youth lying under trees

in marbled solitude, one leg
broken. Nearby, blood-red

poppies and white hemlocks
ripen under a clouded sun.

Santorini Sunset

Before the bright blue domes
and sugar cube houses

melt into the encircling sea,
a recent Chinese bride

poses in white taffeta,
creating her second illusion.

Santorini Concertina

As tourists stroll along
from one spectacular view

to another, a young boy
propped against a whitewashed

wall plays "Never on Sunday"
over and over again.

In Amorgos

Another of Mary's miracles,
the story goes: hammer

and icon gone, then found
high up on a seaside cliff—

so men hewed out a monastery.
Sounds like a trick of Zeus's.

John at Patmos

How could the ancient evangelist,
sleeping with head wedged

into a rock niche, not imagine
his God spoke to him

through the thrice-cracked ceiling
of that spider-ridden cave?

Istanbul Selfie

Hot day in late April,
Hagia Sophia as backdrop—

short-sleeved husband extends
arm, frames photo, grins,

wife, covered head to toe
in black, moon-faced, obliges.

Istanbul Mosques

Brodsky, bitter about backward Ottoman
influences on his native Russia,

called the Blue Mosque a squat toad.
Would he now tag minaretted Suleymaniye Mosque,

overlooking the Bosphorus on its hilltop,
Jabba the Hutt with Tatooine missiles?

Tributes

El Calaboz: Fences and Neighbors

There are bones in the earth all through
this land, animal and human, pulled
by thirst to the river, life dear
and cheap, both, an unforgiving stretch
of humid heat and fateful appetites.

Some have stayed the long course,
raising cattle and corn, raising
one generation, then another,
as the river thins and floods,
taking its bounty on to the sea.

No one threatens this land now
more than before, despite
the towering September horrors
we all lived through, the dust there
part of the dust we breathe here.

Those who cross the river along
this bank pledge their pesos
for a chance to work for wages,
earn a new hope for those behind,
tending ejidos and tiendas, waiting.

One voice held back the bulldozers
for a year. Now the land absorbs
the hammering blows, impaled
and bifurcated, the steel bars
mocking Frost's mocking poem.

Early morning, small birds cross
the river from mesquite to mesquite,
singing the day awake. A hawk
drops to the top rail and commands
silence across this failed dichotomy.

Brutus Abroad

I had hoped to see you one time more, trade poems
and friendly jokes, listen to you tell of your journeys
across continents and ideologies, but I am left now
with memories and shards from your travels,
words that cut or heal as needed, gifts to those
who lived your time and those who are following
in their own time, the young perhaps not ready
to know yet what it meant to be banned, shot
in the back, imprisoned, a wanderer in exile,
but your testimonies will tell them when they
are ready about living widely and loving fully,
great troubadour who sang for us all.

Aftershock
for Bill Pursley

Within the gorgeous landscape
of the heart, there is no sound
that can astonish like that absent
echo. Now no crow is cawing,
no movement through the underbrush,
no smell of earth or bitter taste
of turning berries. The blood is gone
from the air, gone into the grass
that still leans in the moonlight,
where I know as much as I can
ever know, the view almost familiar,
but who can put a finger on the thing
that changes everything, at once,
factoring out this equation's voice
and handshake and web of common
moments? The tremors along the bones
of memory bring me back to the pulse
that I will move to, taking an old friend's
laugh into the dark and the light, both,
as far and long as I can carry them.

For Glen Sorestad

Some of my poems
have traveled across
the border and spoken
right back to yours

summoned by your
frozen First Nations
casualty or the sheer
exuberance of snow

they have admired
your measured voice
and then become
another verse or two

as day declines
to dark and words
are the sparks
that keep us awake

Portrait at Frank's Place

Spare portrait room, open bay windows:
kids in row house across street
chatter with dad, evangelists at end
of block exhort Latino bystanders
to embrace Jesus next to tables
stocked with Marxist tracts. Here
you and I, friends in college,
roommates twice in Austin, brothers
for thirty years to each other's
brothers, talk again of what we
know and do not know, your hand
dipping brush in water and paint,
tricking light on thick paper
to take shape and heft of human
form, on through a final round
of flickering strokes, and then
with my wife and son we drive
across the bay to Buddy's home,
sun disappearing out beyond
Muir Woods, feasting on walls
bearing your paintings and on
your brother's grilled communion.

Travels with Marko

I haven't listened to your songs
in a long time, the homemade cassette
in a box with Dylan, the Stones,

the other sounds that galvanized life
once. Days as liquid as the last tune,
first light framing an open road—

when you got lost you sang your way
to safety, friends and books and dogs
nearby, sadness a string to pluck

and a sound to shape into a song
you could sing again and again,
in a cramped room in San Francisco

or by your van in open country,
the night's constellations telling stories,
the lone coyote telling one too.

When your son asks about your life
back then, pull out your untuned guitar
and pull him into the melancholic

chords that caught rocks and rainwater
and left you free to get up early,
feed the dogs, and drive on, farther.

Raymonda, 1975

I traded Houston's heat
for Jones Hall's chill

as the cast assembled
for afternoon class,

Nureyev striding in,
sweatered and legginged,

toweled at the neck,
teasing pal Erik Bruhn,

slowly tuning for what
still mattered most.

Later, the stage sparked
with orchestrated spins

and elastic ensembles,
Cynthia Gregory's suitor

stalked from wing to wing,
no longer able to hold

the air breathless with leaps,
but like a dark star

he drew us in close
and then shook his mane;

with a single opened arm
he lit up a universe

of body and sound, singeing
the marrow of the moment,

electrons still surging far
beyond the fact of his death.

Umpteenth Operation

No track
star now:

back pain
still constant,

can't keep
food down;

third wife
edgy, edgy.

Gruff laugh
keeps sons

counting on
his grit—

too many
tales begging

to be
told again.

December Walk with Gene

We left your house
before sunrise, streets wet
with a rare misting.

Striding into downtown traffic,
talking about books again,
passing men wanting work.

Café breakfast, spacious station
for buses—now open,
royal palms rising nearby.

Brief stops for chats:
articulate electrician's boyhood
passion for broken appliances,

city planner at a keyshop,
mechanic near a meat market,
frail lady gathering litter.

Voice of the neighborhood,
leading by bamboo staff,
you thumped us homeward.

Billy Collins and Garrison Keillor in the Poetry Ring

Collins and Keillor planned to meet
one spring somewhere in Kentucky—
a poetry smackdown, sneaky Keillor
riffling through his sheaf of sonnets, hoping
to catch Collins off guard, overconfident,
springing some erotic north woods
interlude on his unsuspecting foe,
but I'd put my money on the man
who undressed Dickinson in verse,
tulle tippet a breeze but fumbling at her corset,
unless that poem is stuck behind the one
three thousand miles from Tintern Abbey,
in which case I'd throw in the towel and let
Keillor go out in a blaze of glibness.

Gravity's End

Rescuing Strangers from the Dead

They cannot say what they would
want us to know about them, or if
they would even care, the years
a colorless blank beyond breath,
impressions on those they loved
absorbed by the thirsty earth,
compacted into gritty veins of time.

Wherever we dig we can turn up
a footstep, a shadow, a voice,
a bone, a thing handmade, words
following other words across
a printed page, finding enough
to recognize our own faces
in the fractured light of day.

These Brittle Prints

They were a different couple then,
smiling shyly on the steps of a white
boardinghouse in one, next to a black
Model T in another, staring across
a deserted landscape, somewhere
west of San Angelo, trying to read
what the looming clouds might mean.
By the time they emerged in color,
he was blind and kept to his radio,
she was broad and dipped snuff.

Sorting through their stories about Son
and his older sister, I finally found
Dad there in that windswept world,
peering out from the back window,
hoping to reach the Pecos by afternoon
and catch his first fish, the one
he's holding like a bar of silver,
feet apart, squinting against the future.

Christmas Tree Rings

A cold sunny new year's start,
and we'd split up and scoured
the alleys, snagging pines and firs,
still tinseled or flocked white or pink,
dragging them into our backyards,
fashioning forts to be defended:
bloodthirsty yells, rapid attacks,
wrestling for life on the dead grass.
When darkness finally drove us inside,
our mothers fixed mugs of cocoa
and listened to us chatter on
about our cooked-up conquests.
With green and ever rising sap,
we never imagined our roots
would be severed, the alleys closed,
the forts surrounded by strangers.

Lasting Gift

They are the binoculars
that trained my eyes
to know that a bird
or a tree or a person
contains a thousand
shapes simultaneously,
its field marks shifting
by light and distance
and time of day, both
one thing and many others,
what it was and what
it will become, what
I know just a rounding
off of complexities.

They gave me whatever
range and depth of field
and clarity I bring now
to the things I see
and can't see, day by night,
taking measure through
their two perspectives,
their distinctive voices
and emotions, and finding
therein my own focus.

Inventory for Moving 1
for my father

Take the blackthorn walking stick, though you don't need it yet.
Leave the bunched-waist pants from the thirty pounds of illness.
Take the fine furniture you made—the grand display cabinet, the
    compact writing desk, Mom's dressing table—
and leave the power saw that sliced off two of your fingers on your
    oldest grandson's birthday.
Take your recollections and CDs of Glenn Miller's music
and leave the cars parked in the carport.
Take the annual vacation photo albums, your grown children and their
    spouses seasoning while their babies become young men,
and leave the hiking boots you last wore in the mountains of southern
    Colorado fishing for stocked trout with fellow newsman Max.
Take the naval awards and ribbons and certificates
and leave the Japanese ceremonial sword.
Take the wall plaque engraved with your front-page layout of Neil
    Armstrong's moon walk
and leave the shelves of historical biographies and contemporary
    memoirs you reviewed to supplement reporter wages, fifty-odd
    years back.
Take your wife's hand and walk through the door into new rooms that
    will fill with all your faltering memories.
Leave behind the empty shell you have emerged from.

Inventory for Moving 2
for my mother

Take your fat cat Sam, his cardboard scratch box, and the rabbit
    figurines Dad has given you through the years.
Leave the backyard choir of grackles and blue jays and mourning doves.
Take a couple of wine glasses and a three-meal appetite,
and leave the dishes and cookbooks, the cramped pantry, the drawers of
    kitchen gadgets.
Take the Connecticut spoon collection and glass case of ancestral
    mementos,
and leave the antique bed and antique sofa and antique chairs too frail
    to sit on.
Take the pastel portraits and still lifes you fashioned amid the flux of
    daily meals and housework and carpooling,
and leave the potted geraniums and blue wisteria and pear trees
    snowing in March, filling the patio and driveway with early
    promises.
Take your box of jewelry and framed photographs, loved ones locked
    into their more innocent selves,
and leave the mop and vacuum, broom and toilet brush, iron and oven
    cleaner.
Take your husband's hand and walk through the door into new rooms
    that will fill with all your faltering memories.
Leave behind the empty shell you have emerged from.

Final Song

At ninety
their friends

had been
obituaried

cars gone
home sold

at least
they could

link arms
like two

swing dancers
stepping into

a ballroom
the band

playing its
final song

Omen

Dark bird on a willow limb
against the dappled evening current—
as the curved moon rises
I think of my late father,
telling stories on the porch,
keeping small deaths at bay.

Visit Back Home

Early morning
winter rain

coffee dripping
into daylight

Mom's asleep
across town

when she wakes
she won't remember

where she lived
the last time

her window filled
with empty drizzle.

Holy Chihuly!

Dallas Arboretum, early November

Walkways are lined with more pumpkins
than any kid can conceive of,
zigging through pumpkin-and-gourd houses,
not far from a blue glass starburst.

Past all the pumpkins is one garden
after another after another, greenish
glass ferns rising here, and over there,
by Japanese maples, a sinuous crown
of orange and yellow sunbursts.

This pond contains batches of milky
water lilies, black edged, waiting
for the dark to draw forth the frogs;
that one holds a boat of large spheres,
their jeweled colors celebrating the sun
that keeps us cooling in the shade,
three aging siblings absorbing a view
that our mother, shuffling between rooms
during our visit this morning
to her Alzheimer's floor, will never see.

I'll bet Chihuly would warm to
her orange still life of oranges,
hanging now in my living room,
full of light and just begging
to be peeled, sectioned, and eaten.

Mama Buddha

Amid the wrinkled women and sunlit
hothouse blooms she waits in a wheelchair
for a pianist to play old standards,
and I wonder where she is wandering,
Mama Buddha centering my life
as the world tilts toward the forties,
New York nights and wartime love,
the link to the effervescent click
of who and now and yes yes yes,
a young world full of daily terror,
and now I sit and rub her hands
with lotion, kneading them softly
with old words, the touch of skin
to kindred skin all I can hope to heal.

On the Third Floor

Welcome to their world: up the elevator,
punch in 1300 from the glassed-in vestibule.
A thin woman looks up from her walker
and smiles wanly as two caretakers
chat on their way into the kitchen.
Nearby, several residents on the couch
nap through a black-and-white movie.

Eleven fifteen, and the dining tables
are nearly full of their foursomes,
waiting for another meal they have no
particular appetite for. Rose lights up
as you approach, an aging elf, chattering
her charming gibberish. Margot welcomes
your touch, smiling, says she's doing fine.

Mom sits with eyes closed, still weak
from her cold and a persistent cough,
wheelchair bound. Maxine scowls
at you as usual, perhaps resentful
of attention given to the others,
perhaps locked into an old pattern
she now knows nothing about.

As you massage Mom's hands
with lotion and tell her how much
you love her, even though she may
not hear, hearing aids lost again,
Hannah starts her shouting: "Don't
let the guards take me away!" as she
relives her Auschwitz days once more.

Later you encounter Jack, a new guy,
agile and alert, who has lots
of juice, talks like he almost knows
what he knows, almost slips out

with departing visitors, but without
keying in 1964—likely a good year,
better than this one—he stays put.

     * * *

Six weeks later: the call you know
would come, Mom's inevitable decline.
Body giving up at last, hospice care
around the clock. Her friends stop by,
feeling that something is happening.
Mary Ann taps the door, slips in,
keeps a lengthy feline vigil.

Mom's eyes open but don't focus
when you bend over and whisper
into her good ear. Hard to watch her
go without food and water as she
wished, well along on the journey
only she can take now, floating
on the shallow breathes of being.

They tell you that a half dozen or so
have gone this winter: Hannah
can't feel her pain any longer,
and sweet Rose's son took the call
and then procrastinated so long
the staff had to contact the city morgue
to take away her unclaimed body.

When it's over at last, and you
are taking away the last talismans
that Mom lived with, you pause
and take in this home that she left,
not yours, but hers, a place of light
and care, and bless her for bringing
life three times into her living.

www.ingramcontent.com/pod-product-compliance
Lightning Source LLC
Chambersburg PA
CBHW020945090426
42736CB00010B/1269